RIVER MONSTERS

MARIA L LOPES.

ALEXANDROS POLITIS LOPES

RIVER MONSTERS

ATLANTIC OCEAN

VENEZUELA

GUYANA

SURINAME

FRENCH GUIANA

COLOMBIA

CUADOR

PERU

Rio Negro

Amazon

Belem

Manaus

Natal

Rio Madeira

Rio Xingu

Rio Tocantins

São Francisco

BRASILIA

BOLIVIA

Amazon River

The Amazon River is found in South America. It is the second longest river in the world: a wide and watery highway that the local people travel along. Roads are nonexistent. Its length is approximately 6,400 kilometers (4,000 miles). Humid, and with daily downpours, this mighty river, and the surrounding rainforest, is steeped in ancient mysteries. Many bizarre fish and animals call it their home. The Amazon River also brings in the stuff of modern civilization, forever changing the way its native people live.

The Amazon rainforest receives around nine feet of rain each year (2.7 meters). In the rainy season, the forest is deluged with between 152-157 centimetres. In the dry season, the forest receives a mere 76-245 centimeters. All of this rain, combined with temperatures of 80-90 degrees, contributes to very high humidity during the day. The nights are much more comfortable at around 50 degrees.

May to September is the Amazon's winter, with less rain and cooler temperatures.

The people of the Amazon rainforest use the river to bring in the goods they need, and to send out what they produce - making money for the extras they desire from modern society.

Some people live in floating houseboats made of wood. The strength and durability of the wood used is essential. These people are on the move every day.

A variety of tribes call the Amazon home, with more than a hundred different spoken languages and dialects. Some of these tribes live isolated lives, deep in the jungle, separated from the influence of modern societies. They hunt, fish, and gather jungle fruits and roots. They live in malocas (communal houses) made of straw.

Many of these tribes are content to live off the jungle's bounty. The Kanamari, Kazinawa, Matis, Waimini and Marubo, for instance, tap the rubber trees and sell the rubber. The earnings are either spent on treats not found hanging from the jungle trees, or traded for goods they need.

Interestingly, the Tacuna tribe is not afraid to mingle with the outside people they meet. They haggle, barter, and sell a variety of crafts. Talented and artistic, they make clothing from palm tree leaves and colourful bird feathers. They also use the palm leaves to weave baskets. Their carvings are traditional, and made from brazilwood, which is a Brazilian tree. It has a dense, orange-red wood.

This mysterious river does not give up its secrets easily. Hidden dangers lurk in its black waters, hang from its branches, and drink from its shores, including the howler monkey, jaguar and emerald tree boa.

The world within the depths of the Amazon River is teeming with life, with over 3,000 known species of fish, from the tiniest Neon Tetra, to the most feared Piranha, to many others that are much bigger and scarier. More species are constantly being discovered.

RiVeR DoLPHiN

Let's begin with a really gentle biggie: The Amazon River dolphin is the largest freshwater dolphin, and the most elusive creature in the river. In the murky waters of the Amazon, this dolphin had no need for eyes. It relies on delicate and fine tuned whiskers. These whiskers are used for echolocation, allowing the dolphin to safely navigate through the river.

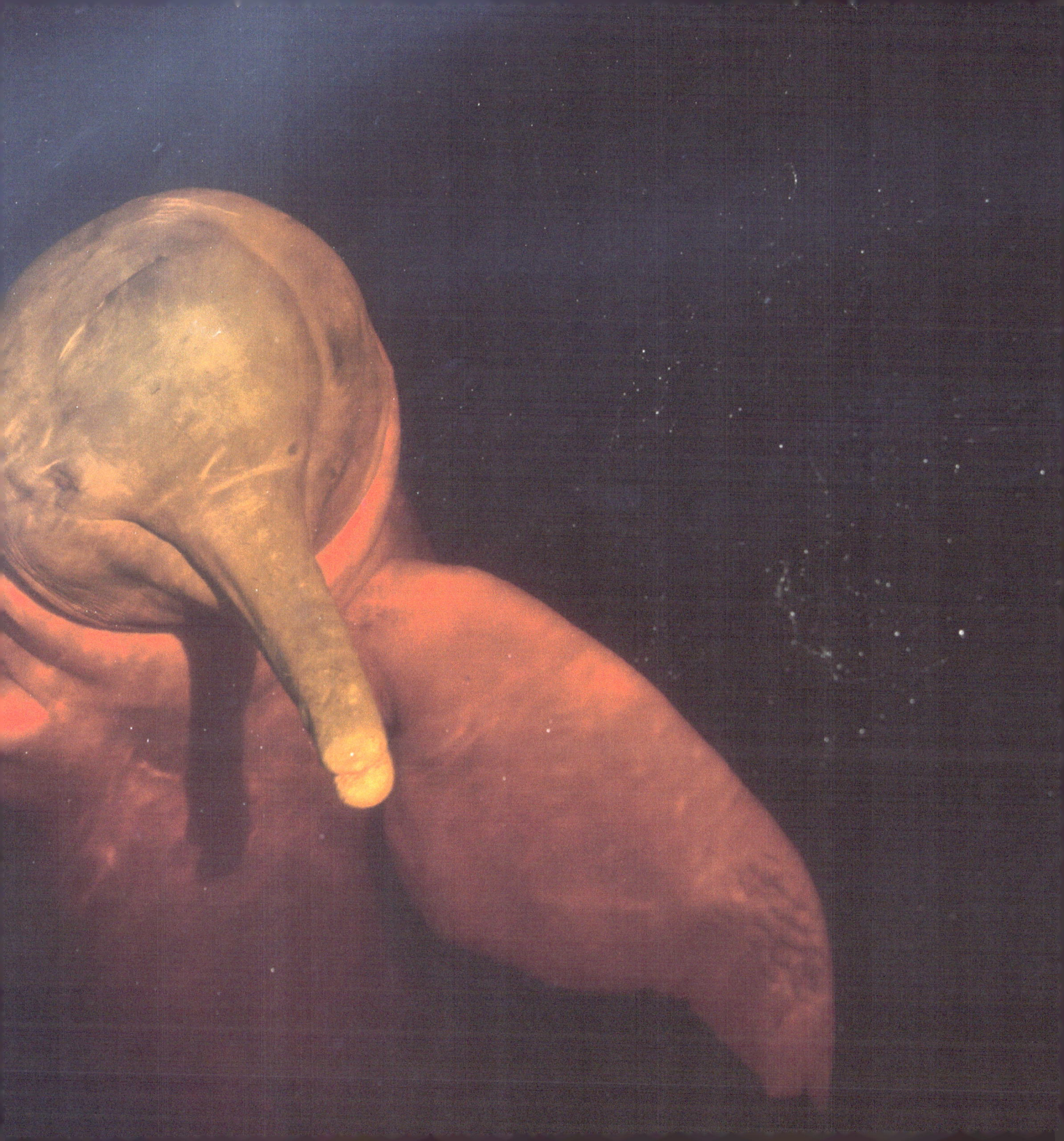

ANACONDA

Now for the slithery, scary, giant anaconda, the fiercest snake in the world. Happy on land, in water, or dangling from a tree... waiting for dinner! They kill by coiling around a prospective meal, and giving the creature a BIG l-o-n-g squeeze until the victim suffocates. They can squeeze a human to death. So remember, if you hug an anaconda, it WILL hug back!

CAIMAN

Caiman are common in the Amazon River. Baby caiman make a distress call (a popping sound) to alert their mum when they are threatened by predators. Dwarf caimans are the smallest of the species, around 1.3 - 1.5 metres (4.3 to 4.9 feet) in length. The largest is the black caiman, 1.72 metres (5.6 feet) in length. Their natural predators are jaguar and anaconda. However, humans top their kill list.

Pike Cichlids

Pike cichlids are fish that take childcare very seriously. When danger threatens, the babies swarm into Mama's mouth. They hide there until it is safe to swim out. Pike cichlids have a different behaviour to the rest of their fishy family. They dine by catching insects.

BLACK GHOST

The black ghost fish will never be a stand-up comedian. It is nocturnal and shy, and communicates by making vibrations in the water. The indigenous people believe that the black ghost fish takes over their spirit when they die. This belief makes it a holy fish in the eyes of the local tribes. So, if you catch one, throw it back. Or you might offend a local tribe.

STINGRAY

The freshwater stingray has a 12 to 15-inch poisonous barb in its tail. But not to worry, they only sting in self-defence. One zap of their tail can drown a diver. As a bottom dweller, it feeds on snails and crabs. An interesting fact from Greek history: they used the venom from the stingray's spine as an anesthetic.

Needle Fish

Needle fish are as old as dirt - prehistoric in fact. It is a predatory fish from the Mesozoic Era, Cretaceous period, around 135-65 million years ago. Their common name is "garfish." They are timid and skittish, and range in size from 3 centimetres (1.2 inches) in width to 95 centimetres (37 inches) in length. They hunt day and night. When frightened or endangered, the needle fish make popping sounds that hopefully scare off predators. They enjoy dining on small fish and crustaceans. If you want a contender for the Olympic long jump, the needle fish might be a good choice. They can jump very long distances.

ARAPAIMA

Arapaima are the largest freshwater fish in the Amazon River, and they must surface to breathe. This fish has been around since the age of the dinosaur. Their "bony" tongue is fitted with a set of teeth. The indigenous people sometimes carve the Arapaima's teeth into tools for hunting and fishing. Legend says that Arapaima was an Indian who belonged to the Uaías tribe. He was a brave but heartless warrior. The God of Thunder punished him by sentencing him to live forever in the Amazon waters as a giant dark fish.

ELECTRIC EEL

Electric eels have a reputation for killing humans and animals. They can knock out their prey with one lethal high voltage discharge (about 600 volts). A zap from an Electric eel can kill a man, or knock a horse off its feet.

PANAQUE

Panaque are the only fish that eat wood. This fish can be found in fast-flowing streams during the rainy season. The Panaque loves to lurk around tree roots, and within log piles close to river banks. This huge monster is a gentle creature and harmless to humans. It is known as a canoe eater as they have a habit of chewing holes in wooden canoes.

PiRANHa

Piranahs? Oh yes, a word of warning. Never invite a piranha to dinner unless you plan to feed it well. The piranha is a river scavenger with a fierce reputation. They are cannibals. If food is scarce, they have no problem with eating each other. Like sharks, they have a sensory ability to detect fresh blood in the water. To the piranha, the smell of fresh blood is the dinner bell!

CANDIRU
ASU

Candiru asu is the tiniest of vertebrates from the same family as the toothpick fish. It has small sharp teeth and is one of the most industrious of scavengers. Working as a parasite on other fish, it enters a host's body through their gills. Swim if you dare, because it can enter the human body as well.

CATFISH

The giant wild freshwater catfish are bottom feeders. They use their sensitive whiskers to locate food on the river bottom. Small animals, frogs, and insects are also on their menu. The catfish has lungs, so it can breathe out of water. They crawl out of the water on their front fins, and push themselves along with help from their tail. If you bump into a catfish in the mud beside the Amazon River – RUN! These Catfish can reach around 10 feet (3 meters) in length, and weight up to 450 pounds (200 kilograms). Run fast!

MANaTee

The manatee is a friendly creature –
just the sort to make a great neighbour.
They are large mammals that swim
slowly in the Amazon's coastal waters
and rivers. Local legend has it that
they were once human. Some tribes
think they are related to mermaids.
Traditional African culture has made
them sacred.

The Amazon River begins in Solimões das águas and ends where it pours into the Atlantic Ocean. At low water, the mouth of the Amazon River has an immense width. It is camouflaged by various islands that divide the river mouth into arms called paraná. As the Amazon wanders through the lush and humid rain forest, many rivers, both large and small, join it. These multiple rivers add great diversity to the Amazon River's length and width. The largest of these, a huge river in its own right, is the Rio Negro. When these two mighty rivers come together, the mixing of their waters becomes a grand and beautiful natural spectacle.

If you are fortunate enough to visit the Amazon River and its surrounding rain forest, bring your camera. Many wild, wonderful, and amazing sights await the click of your finger.

WORD GLOSSARY

Temperate = Places where it is neither very hot nor very cold, usually with warm summers and cool winters.

Murky Water = The river looks dark or dirty, due to flooding or strong currents.

Deluge = A large flood or heavy fall of rain.

Rubber Tree = A tree that produces a strong elastic substance used for making tyres, balls, hoses, and other things.

Dialects = A language used by people in one area of the country but not the rest of the country.

Invertebrates = Spineless creatures that live in oceans or rivers: coral, crabs, snails, sponges, and the like.

Camouflage = Colours and patterns that blend with the surroundings, making a creature hard to see.

Predator = An animals that hunts others for food.

Endanger species = A type of animal or plant that has become so rare that it is danger of becoming extinct.

Some other books by **Maria L. Lopes**

A Good Scare!

This is a message that has universal appeal, and presenting it with loveable animal characters makes the essence of the story accessible to even the youngest of children.

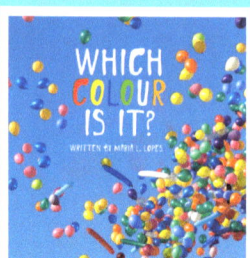

Which Colour is it?

Which Colour Is It? is a book that is aimed at very young children.
The bright colours and pictures are designed to develop language awareness.
Each page of the book is filled with colours, words and objects that begin with the same letter of the alphabet.
Babies and toddlers will be eager to explore every page of the book.

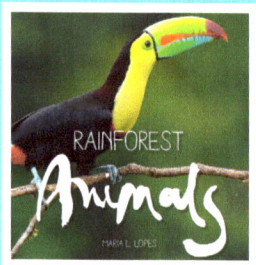

Rainforest Animals

Brings readers up close with rainforest animals that are in danger of extinction due to loss habitat.
Young children will enjoy exploring every page of this book.

Boogie Woogie Woo

In *Boogie Woogie Woo*, we meet a young boy and his pet mouse who love to perform their favourite songs by tapping and singing. They take the music out to the street, greeting everyone they meet.

www.MariasChildrensBooks.com

www.ingramcontent.com/pod-product-compliance
Lightning Source LLC
Chambersburg PA
CBHW041514280526
45792CB00004B/1252